BELONGING

Accessibility, Inclusion, and Christian Community

LifeGuide® BIBLE STUDIES

DEBORAH MEYER ABBS

IVP

An imprint of InterVarsity Press
Downers Grove, Illinois

InterVarsity Press
P.O. Box 1400, Downers Grove, IL 60515-1426
ivpress.com
email@ivpress.com

InterVarsity Press® is the book-publishing division of InterVarsity Christian Fellowship/USA®, a movement of students and faculty active on campus at hundreds of universities, colleges, and schools of nursing in the United States of America, and a member movement of the International Fellowship of Evangelical Students. For information about local and regional activities, visit intervarsity.org.

While any stories in this book are true, some names and identifying information may have been changed to protect the privacy of individuals.

Cover design and image composite: David Fassett
Interior design: Jeanna Wiggins
Image: welcome on a cork board: © mattjeacock / E+ / Getty Images

ISBN 978-0-8308-3156-2 (print)
ISBN 978-0-8308-3157-9 (digital)

Printed in the United States of America ♾

InterVarsity Press is committed to ecological stewardship and to the conservation of natural resources in all our operations. This book was printed using sustainably sourced paper.

P 25 24 23 22 21 20 19 18 17 16 15 14 13 12 11 10 9 8 7 6 5 4 3 2 1
Y 37 36 35 34 33 32 31 30 29 28 27 26 25 24 23 22 21

CONTENTS

GETTING THE MOST OUT OF *BELONGING*

A **while back my friend** John and I shared a meal at one of my favorite hamburger joints. We discussed a variety of topics, but what I remember most revolved around the deep need we all have for a place of belonging.

John said, "The best thing to do when thinking about a Bible study or other group that includes those with disabilities is to make the person feel welcomed, that they belong and will be able to use their God-given gifts to make a contribution."

John is highly intelligent and has the ability to focus intensely on a problem from every angle until he comes up with a solution. Being on the autism spectrum, he understands the barriers to belonging that can arise from having an invisible disability.

I'm not going out on a limb in thinking that everyone on the planet has experienced loneliness and a lack of belonging at some point. For those with either visible or invisible disabilities, however, this is often more than a passing phase and can affect us at a deep, spiritual level. It's not just architecture that causes exclusion but also attitudes and ableism. While usually less discussed than racism or sexism, ableism similarly labels an entire group of people—those with disabilities—as less-than through disregard, devaluation, and discrimination.

Laura, who earned a degree in biochemistry from the University of California–Santa Cruz, was literally sitting in a tree outside her church one Sunday. When the worship music was uncharacteristically loud, she had to get to a quieter location. Laura also attended the 2018 Urbana Missions Conference with more than seventeen thousand others, and having a sensory lounge available there during the plenary sessions really helped. She had somewhere to go to be welcomed, belong, and still be in community.

As Tom Lin, president of InterVarsity Christian Fellowship/USA, explains, "Belonging is how God meant for us to live. We are wired for relationship—with him and each other. Connection and community are necessary conditions for healthy, thriving human life."[1] In my own faith journey and for many of us, friendship with Jesus starts and grows from being included in community.

But what about the 61 million adults (one in four) and 19 percent of college undergraduates in the United States who have a documented disability? Often they aren't represented or able to find acceptance, community, and places to use their gifts in our churches, youth ministries, or campus groups.

One common hindrance to belonging is the attitude that those without disabilities assist and serve those with disabilities, but not vice versa—that it's a one-way street. This is a dangerous assumption and simply not true; we are colaborers who serve one another. We all lose out when part of the body of Christ is missing and unable to use their spiritual gifts. God's kingdom includes us all, and how wonderfully diverse it is!

My wonderful, athletic youngest son, Luke, needs a lot of support with daily living skills due to his disability, but don't assume he doesn't have his own faith in Jesus or spiritual gifts. Even though he can't speak, he communicates, is smart, and gets his point across.

Luke and Noah became friends when Noah and his parents began assisting Luke in Sunday school through Masterpiece Ministry at Chapelstreet Church. They are alike in being fidgety and enjoying movement but also good at chilling out when the time is right. It's a reciprocal relationship.

"Luke's a good friend of mine and made me realize a lot of things about myself I never would have known or figured out if I didn't meet him," said Noah. His mom and dad speak the truth when they say Luke ministers to Noah. It's kingdom work, and it works both ways.

May these nine Bible studies help us know the deep love and acceptance of our heavenly Father and as a result offer acceptance and love to one another. It's my hope that this study helps you on the journey of accessibility. It can be used by accessible, integrated small groups or by groups or individuals who want to see how Jesus responds in love to those who are often marginalized and excluded. The goal is that we can follow in his footsteps and welcome people of all abilities.

SUGGESTIONS FOR INDIVIDUAL STUDY

1. As you begin each study, pray that God will speak to you through his Word.

2. Read the introduction to the study and respond to the personal reflection question or exercise. This is designed to help you focus on God and on the theme of the study.

3. Each study deals with a particular passage—so that you can delve into the author's meaning in that context. Read and reread the passage to be studied. The questions are written using the language of the New International Version, so you may wish to use that version of the Bible. The New Revised Standard Version is also recommended.

4. This is an inductive Bible study, designed to help you discover for yourself what Scripture is saying. The study includes three types of questions. *Observation* questions ask about the basic facts: who, what, when, where, and how. *Interpretation* questions delve into the meaning of the passage. *Application* questions help you discover the implications of the text for growing in Christ. These three keys unlock the treasures of Scripture.

Write your answers to the questions in the spaces provided or in a personal journal. Writing can bring clarity and deeper understanding of yourself and of God's Word.

5. It might be good to have a Bible dictionary handy. Use it to look up any unfamiliar words, names, or places.

6. Use the prayer suggestion to guide you in thanking God for what you have learned and to pray about the applications that have come to mind.

7. You may want to go on to the suggestion under "Now or Later," or you may want to use that idea for your next study.

SUGGESTIONS FOR MEMBERS OF A GROUP STUDY

1. Come to the study prepared. Follow the suggestions for individual study mentioned above. You will find that careful preparation will greatly enrich your time spent in group discussion.

2. Be willing to participate in the discussion. The leader of your group will not be lecturing. Instead, he or she will be encouraging the members of the group to discuss what they have learned. The leader will be asking the questions that are found in this guide.

3. Stick to the topic being discussed. Your answers should be based on the verses which are the focus of the discussion and not on outside authorities such as commentaries or speakers. These studies focus on a particular passage of Scripture. Only rarely should you refer to other portions of the Bible. This allows for everyone to participate in in-depth study on equal ground.

4. Be sensitive to the other members of the group. Listen attentively when they describe what they have learned. You may be surprised by their insights! Each question assumes a variety of answers. Many questions do not have "right" answers, particularly questions that aim at meaning or application. Instead the questions push us to explore the passage more thoroughly.

When possible, link what you say to the comments of others. Also, be affirming whenever you can. This will encourage some of the more hesitant members of the group to participate.

5. Be careful not to dominate the discussion. We are sometimes so eager to express our thoughts that we leave too little opportunity for others to respond. By all means participate! But allow others to also.

6. Expect God to teach you through the passage being discussed and through the other members of the group. Pray that you will have an enjoyable and profitable time together, but also that as a result of the study you will find ways that you can take action individually and/or as a group.

7. Remember that anything said in the group is considered confidential and should not be discussed outside the group unless specific permission is given to do so.

8. If you are the group leader, you will find additional suggestions at the back of the guide.

---

[1]Tom Lin, InterVarsity fundraising letter, December 2019.

ONE

A TRUE PLACE OF BELONGING AND INCLUSION

Luke 7:36-50

We all long for a place to just ***be***—somewhere we can relax, be our true selves, and be loved unconditionally. Whatever our ability level, each of us has a God-given need for community and a place to belong.

For those of us affected by disability or who have loved ones who are affected, accessibility issues and ableism (bias against people with disabilities) can make it difficult to find that comfortable and comforting place.

This sense of belonging, for each of us, starts with a friendship with God. My son Brandon puts it like this: "I've always known that even if I didn't belong where I was, I'd belong in God's eyes because I'm one of his children and he loves me."

Group Discussion. If you could ask God one question, what would it be? Why is the answer to that question important to you?

Personal Reflection. How would you describe your relationship with God right now?

The Bible shows us the truth about ourselves and Jesus. The Pharisees, who interpreted the law of Moses and lived a life of privilege, often rejected Jesus. In this passage a Pharisee invites Jesus to dinner, and an uninvited guest shows up. *Read Luke 7:36-50.*

1. Who are the main characters in this passage? What do we learn about them and their social statuses?

2. What emotions do you think the woman was experiencing?

3. In light of Simon's position as a Pharisee, describe his likely perspective on this woman and her station in life.

4. Who else did Simon judge besides the woman?

5. Have you ever been judged or looked down on? How did it make you feel?

6. Can you describe a time when you've thought less of someone for their actions, illness, or disability?

7. In the passage we see Jesus talking directly to two people: Simon and the woman. Compare and contrast Jesus' response to each of them.

8. Why do you think Jesus asked Simon, "Do you see this woman?"

9. In verses 44-47, Jesus addresses what Simon needed to understand. How did Simon fail as a host?

10. What did the other guests think about Jesus forgiving the woman's sins, and why?

11. Notice what Jesus says to the woman in verse 50. What do you think hearing these words meant to her?

12. What do Jesus' words here mean to you?

13. Currently, who do you relate to more, the woman or the Pharisee? How does this affect your relationship with Jesus?

Thank the Lord for his generous forgiveness, that he truly sees each of us, and that he gives us himself to belong to forever.

NOW OR LATER

Read John 3:1-21, a familiar text about a Pharisee who seeks out Jesus for answers. Reflect on Jesus' message to Nicodemus (and us) as to how we can belong to him for eternity.

TWO

GOD CREATED US AND KNOWS US

Psalm 139

For some of us, a debilitating disability can come in the form of a mental health diagnosis. This was the case for me when I was pregnant with my oldest son, Brandon, who is now a college student. The hormonal changes early on in the pregnancy caused my brain to get out of whack, and I had a manic episode. After a couple of weeks I crashed. I was so depressed and impaired that I couldn't get out of bed without being forced, nor could I think clearly enough to pick out an outfit or get dressed without the help of my loving husband, spitfire mom, or dear friend Diana.

In the midst of God knitting together a new life inside me, I was unraveling. As the months dragged on I wondered if I'd ever be functional or productive again. And how would I take care of my baby once he arrived when I couldn't even care for myself? I lost all self-confidence and wondered why God bothered to create such a useless person. Thankfully, God's Word tells a much different story about each of us than what my thoughts told me during deep depression.

Group Discussion. Have you ever felt that others had misconceptions about you? How did it make you feel?

Personal Reflection. What things have you believed about yourself that are not true according to God's Word?

Sometimes we don't realize or remember how powerful and ever-present God is. The passage we're studying is a great reminder. Besides learning more about God, we will see the loving way we were each created and what God thinks of us. *Read Psalm 139.*

1. What do we learn about God in verses 1-12?

2. Which verbs describing God's activity jump out to you? Why?

3. What does the writer, David, seem to think about God's omnipresence and power in his life?

How does this help you to trust God more?

4. What do you learn about yourself and others in verses 13-16?

5. At times society and even the church tell us that those with disabilities are less-than. How does this affect our thoughts about ourselves and others?

6. What are some things we can do to help ourselves and others believe and act on the truth in verses 13-16?

7. Verse 16 says God had all of our days written in his book before any of them happened. How does that make you feel?

8. What does David say about the Lord in verses 17-18?

9. How do you think praising God might lead to hating those who hate God?

10. In the final two verses, what does David ask God to do? Why do you think he asks this?

11. When have you made a similar request of God? In what ways has he answered?

Take time to praise God for who he is and thank him for creating you and having all your days planned.

NOW OR LATER

Spend time praying and meditating on the truth about yourself and the Lord in this passage. Write a response back to God.

Another way to sense the nearness of God that David talks about in Psalm 139 is by practicing breath prayer. As you breathe in deeply, repeat any name of the Lord that is meaningful to you. When you exhale, offer up a desire of your heart. Since breath prayer is short, you can practice this as you go about your day. The breath prayer I've been practicing lately is breathing in, "Abba," breathing out, "I belong to you."

THREE

EQUAL ACCESS TO THE FATHER

Ephesians 2:8-22

Historically, and even still today for a whole host of reasons, those with disabilities have been denied access to medical care, mobility, food, education, and other things many people take for granted.

Many of us affected by disability or chronic illness also have a difficult time getting out of the house to be in Christian community. Safety issues, medical conditions, behaviors, and lack of support in some Christian communities are just a few of the barriers we face. For those with compromised health, this reality was brought to an even more critical level with the spread of Covid-19 beginning in 2020.

Thankfully, we still have access to the Lord. We're also seeing how technology can help churches, campus ministries, and other Christian communities move online for encouragement, prayer, Bible study, and connection. Doing virtual church or small groups is one option that can help us, but it certainly does not replace being together in person.

For my family, Chapelstreet Church in Geneva, Illinois, the special needs ministry there called Masterpiece, and Joni and Friends Family Retreats are spots where we have felt belonging. If my son Luke is having a hard time there, I don't need to worry. Why? Because he fits right in and is still invited, welcomed, and loved.

Group Discussion. When and where have you experienced community? What qualities did these people or groups have that gave you a sense of belonging?

Personal Reflection. How has your faith in Jesus given you a place to belong with him?

Because of Jesus' death and resurrection, the apostle Paul writes, *all* people, not only the Jews, can gain entry and be reconciled to both God and one another. In this study, we learn more about what it means to be the people of God and how Jesus has broken down the barrier to include everyone. As sisters and brothers in Christ, we are family. *Read Ephesians 2:8-22.*

1. According to this passage, how are we saved?

2. How should verse 10 shape our view of ourselves and others?

3. Compare the status of the Gentiles in verses 11-12 with that in verse 13.

4. Reread verses 14-17. What did Jesus do, and what was his purpose?

5. How might people with disabilities and those without them need to do the work of reconciliation between their two groups?

6. In verse 17 Paul writes that Jesus preached peace to those near and those far away. How close do you feel in your relationship with Jesus currently?

7. How and why do we have access to the Father?

8. What benefits do God's people receive?

9. Contemplate the shades of meaning in the terms "fellow citizens" and "members of [God's] household" (v. 19). One is more public and one is more intimate. What is implied by these terms, both separately and together?

10. Who makes up the community in this passage?

11. What is the significance of referring to Jesus as the "chief cornerstone"?

12. At the beginning of the study we discussed the characteristics of communities where we experienced belonging. How do those characteristics match up with what Paul is describing in the passage?

Thank the Lord that through Jesus we all have access to him by the Holy Spirit. Ask the Lord to continue breaking down barriers and misunderstandings between groups in the Christian family, especially between those with and without disabilities. If needed, ask God's forgiveness and help to bring reconciliation.

NOW OR LATER

Read Galatians 3:26-29 (I recommend using the NLT version). Here we also see how we are all one in Christ. Reflect in particular on verse 28, and as you feel led write down other categories to add to it, such as, "There is no longer neurotypical or neurodiverse, for you are all one in Christ."

FOUR

WE ALL HAVE A PLACE AT THE TABLE

2 Samuel 9:1-13

When my son Luke left Giant Steps, his private day school for those with autism, to attend Monarch Center for Autism out of state, his friend Tyler gave him the sweetest card ever. He wrote: "I am so so so proud of how far you have come in a year. We have become best friends! I don't know what I am going to do without seeing your smiling face when I help you off the bus. You most definitely have become my best friend. We are two peas in a pod."

Tyler works at Giant Steps, and their friendship grew from there. Tyler has visited Luke for the weekend near his new school and makes sure to see Luke every time he's home on break—and they are both so happy to be together again. Although Tyler is a busy young man working full-time and getting his master's degree, I know he'd be one of the people coming alongside Brandon, Luke's big brother, to make sure Luke has a place at the table, a good home, and community if my husband or I ever couldn't assist.

Group Discussion. Describe a TV show or movie whose characters you would like to befriend and share a meal with.

Personal Reflection. How might God be asking you to use your status or position to help someone else in a practical way?

In this passage King David takes initiative to show hospitality for the sake of his promise to his best friend, Jonathan, after Jonathan and his father, Saul, were killed. *Read 2 Samuel 9:1-13.*

1. What was David's motivation for asking the question in verse 1?

2. Who are the main characters in this passage, and what are some things we learn about them?

3. Describe the scene between David and Mephibosheth in verses 6-8.

4. Why do you think David first told Mephibosheth not to be afraid?

5. Does Mephibosheth's response to David surprise you? Why or why not?

6. In verses 9-13, what words or details stand out to you?

7. What status did eating at David's table give to Mephibosheth?

8. How might this have restored Mephibosheth's view of himself, his identity, and his place in society?

9. The New Testament portrays Jesus as our King who invites us to his table through his death and resurrection. How should this affect our own self-esteem and identity?

10. Have there been times when ableism inside or outside the church has influenced how you see yourself or see others with disabilities? Describe these effects.

11. How might you come alongside, invite, and advocate *with* (not just for) those who are marginalized, as we see David do in this passage?

Pray that you or your small group would take an opportunity to invite someone who might typically be overlooked to join you for a meal or group gathering.

NOW OR LATER

Read Luke 14:15-24. What additional insights does Jesus' parable here provide?

FIVE

A NEW PURPOSE FOR US ALL

Luke 5:1-11

My **friend Jeff,** who grew up on a farm in Minnesota, says, "Following Jesus changed the trajectory of my life and turned it in a totally different direction." When Jeff was about thirteen his pastor asked if he'd ever thought about serving Jesus. Jeff figured maybe he'd start doing that when he was, say, sixty years old.

Clearly God had other ideas. Jeff and his wife, Jane, have served for nearly forty years as missionaries with InterVarsity Christian Fellowship (IVCF) in the United States and with IVCF's sister movement in New Zealand and England. And he isn't even sixty yet! He loves reaching out to college students with the good news of Jesus and helping them dig into God's Word.

For my friend Shari, life's trajectory was changed by a rare neuromuscular disease that affects her mobility. Formerly an electrician, she now has a different kind of ministry. She writes, advocates, creates artwork along with Scripture verses on giant postcards, and prays with others when they request prayer.

God has given both Jeff and Shari a ministry and purpose that they didn't imagine!

Group Discussion. What is it about Jesus that compels you to follow (or not follow) him?

Personal Reflection. Think of a time Jesus asked you to do something you didn't want to do. Where you happy with your response? Why or why not?

Jesus is fantastic at meeting people right where they are and calling them to follow him. In this passage we see Jesus do and say exactly what these fisherman need to be motivated to leave their nets behind and "catch" men and women instead. *Read Luke 5:1-11.*

1. Put your feet in Simon Peter's sandals. Explain what happened at the lake.

2. What strikes you about Simon's response to Jesus' request in verse 5?

3. Think of a time Jesus asked you to take a leap of faith and you were skeptical, like Peter. What was this experience like, and how did it change your view of Jesus?

4. How did Simon Peter and the others view Jesus differently after his display of power with the huge catch? Why?

5. How did Peter see himself differently?

6. Notice what Jesus said at the end of verse 10. How might this reassure and encourage Simon and his companions?

7. What new vocation did Jesus give them?

8. Do you think Simon, James, and John understood what Jesus meant in verse 10?

9. Where in particular has God placed you? How do you think God wants to use you to "fish for people" in your unique location and circumstances?

10. How did the fishermen respond to Jesus' call?

11. What might Jesus be asking you to leave behind as you follow him?

12. What might he be asking you and your friends, family, church, or campus group to let go of to follow him more fully as his community?

13. What kinds of barriers might people put in front of each other that Jesus would not?

Pray for strength to follow hard after Jesus, and ask his help to reach other people so they come to know him too.

NOW OR LATER

Read 1 John 1:9. Are there sins you need to confess, like Peter did, in order to be closer to Jesus and his purposes for your life? Take time to do that; write it in a journal if it helps you to focus. Then spend time praying for friends and family who don't yet know Jesus.

SIX

A DIFFERENT KIND OF HEALING

Mark 2:1-12

When my son Luke was almost three years old, he started to lose his speech. He had been able to say around seventy-five single words and some phrases, such as "Bye-bye, brother" when we dropped big brother, Brandon, at his elementary school. But bit by bit his voice disappeared until he could only say the word *more*.

Then that stopped too.

Shortly after his third birthday our Luke was diagnosed with autism. He's now sixteen and uses a program on his iPad called TouchChat to talk, mostly about the food he wants since he is a foodie like his mama! On rare occasions, when he is very sad or mad, Luke occasionally yells, "No!" Honestly, we love to hear it.

Just because he can't talk doesn't mean he can't *understand* what others are saying, as people sometimes assume. He is a smart guy!

Group Discussion. What questions do you have about faith, disability, and healing?

Personal Reflection. What does it mean to you to have faith in God, even if he doesn't choose to heal you or a loved one emotionally, mentally, or physically?

It's so easy to think that our own disability or illness, or that of a loved one, is what needs healing first and foremost. In this story, Jesus encounters a paralyzed man who needs more than physical healing. Jesus looks beyond his physical disability to examine a more critical need. *Read Mark 2:1-12.*

1. Describe the scene in verses 1-4. What happened when Jesus was teaching?

2. How do you think the paralyzed man felt about needing his friends to bring him to Jesus?

3. When have you invited or needed friends to help you? How did that make you feel?

4. If the paralyzed man and his friends expected Jesus to heal him physically, how do you think they felt when Jesus forgave his sins instead?

5. What has been your experience of asking God to heal you or praying for a friend or family member to be healed?

6. Pretend you're a reporter for the town blog or newspaper. How would you report the scene in verses 5-12?

7. Who objected to what Jesus was doing? What did they take issue with?

8. In this instance, Jesus said he healed the man to show his authority over sin. What might be God's reason for *not* healing an illness or disability?

9. How have you seen God glorified and people brought closer to Christ through someone with a disability or illness?

10. In this passage, the crowd made Jesus inaccessible to the paralyzed man without the extreme measure of making a hole in the roof. Does accessibility need to be improved in your community, church, or group meetings? If so, how can it be improved?

11. How do you respond when you feel God isn't answering your prayers?

12. How has God helped you deal with these feelings?

Ask God to help you praise and trust him both when he does answer prayers and bring healing, and when his answer is no or not yet.

NOW OR LATER

Look back at the passage we studied and think about the faith and action both the paralyzed man and his friends showed. They truly took a risk! Spend time listening to God and journaling as you ask the Lord ways he wants you to take a risk outside your comfort zone.

SEVEN

FOLLOWING JESUS' EXAMPLE OF FORGIVENESS

Luke 23:32-49

In college, Kat was a student leader with InterVarsity. Now she serves as an InterVarsity campus volunteer as well as working in the corporate world. She's married to her college sweetheart, and she has a disability called TAR (thrombocytopenia absent radius) syndrome.

The way Kat was treated in some of her college courses was quite difficult at times. "A few teachers hated my accommodations for schoolwork. Others assumed I needed help and gave me slack when they should not have," Kat said. "These behaviors made me feel less of a student; they made me feel less capable." Finding a job after college has also been more difficult due to prejudices and lack of understanding.

For Kat and for each of us in the Christian family, God calls us to forgive others as he forgives us. This can be especially challenging for those who are part of a marginalized group like the disability community, which for too long has been subject to the unseen, forgotten "ism." Kat said, "I have been realizing that many people don't have any interactions with people with disabilities. Accepting their ignorance and understanding how I can educate them has changed my thoughts on how I should forgive them."

Group Discussion. Talk about a time in your life when people's lack of understanding or even outright bullying has impacted you or someone you love.

Personal Reflection. Bring your feelings and thoughts about experiences of mistreatment to God. Ask him for healing and to help you forgive.

Before Jesus was nailed to the cross, he had already endured betrayal, mockery, beatings, and abuse. Simon from Cyrene was made to carry the cross behind Jesus, and women mourned for him. We pick up the story here. *Read Luke 23:32-49.*

1. Describe the scene in verses 32-43. Who was present?

2. If you were a bystander at the crucifixion, what suffering would you see Jesus experience on the cross?

3. How did Jesus respond to the people responsible for putting him to death?

4. Compare how the two criminals interacted with Jesus. What did the repentant criminal ask of him?

5. How do you feel about Jesus' response to the repentant criminal?

6. If you knew your death was imminent, what would you say to God?

7. When has it been difficult for you to forgive someone who has hurt or misjudged you or a loved one?

8. What do you think empowered Jesus to offer forgiveness?

9. Describe what happened in verses 44-46 and its significance.

10. What was the response of the centurion? Why?

11. How does Jesus' death on the cross and forgiving his executioners motivate you to forgive others?

Pray and thank the Lord for enduring death on the cross to forgive us. Pray for one another to be able to forgive those who have wronged you as Christ has forgiven you.

NOW OR LATER

Knowing God's lavish love for us and having it sink deep into our hearts and minds is a lifelong process. Meditate on Paul's prayer in Ephesians 3:14-21. What a rich passage it is! Then read Ephesians 4:32 and ask God to help you live it out.

EIGHT

GOD'S POWER DISPLAYED IN A MAN BORN BLIND

John 9:1-41

In some parts of the world, people with disabilities are still routinely hidden away and excluded from their communities because their life is thought to be worth less. This may have been the fate of my friend Michael had God not intervened in remarkable ways.

Michael survived a civil war in Sudan as a young boy. Then, after he contracted a disease that could have been fatal, God used a Kenyan surgeon and a missionary doctor to save his life. After hearing about Jesus while hospitalized, Michael received Christ. On top of that, God spoke to the wife of the missionary doctor saying they should adopt Michael, giving him the chance to go to school and attend college. Amazing, right?

And the story doesn't end there! Michael, who as a result of his illness is a wheelchair user, felt called by God to return to Kenya to offer hope in Christ to others in a similar situation. So far, through his ministry called Living with Hope more than a thousand people have heard the good news about Jesus and been given the gift of mobility.

Group Discussion. Describe a time you've seen the work of God displayed in someone's life.

Personal Reflection. In what ways do you struggle with seeing God at work in your own life?

Jesus shows his disciples a new way of thinking about disability in this passage, which centers on a man with visual impairment and Jesus' interaction with him. It also points out Jesus' bigger concern: spiritual blindness. *Read John 9:1-41.*

1. Why do you think the disciples asked Jesus the question in verse 2?

2. How did Jesus respond?

3. Describe what Jesus did—and asked the man to do—to give him sight. Why do you think Jesus did this?

4. How did the different groups in the story respond to Jesus healing the man?

5. Imagine yourself at the scene. How do you think you would have responded to Jesus giving sight to the man?

6. How do you explain the differing replies of the man and of his parents when the Pharisees question them?

7. Have you ever had a family member or friend bail on you like the healed man's parents did? Describe how it made you feel.

8. How does or would it help to have an ally who advocates alongside you?

9. Look at the interplay between the man and the Pharisees in verses 24-34. What stands out to you?

10. What did Jesus do when he heard the man had been thrown out?

11. Compare the man's response to Jesus with the Pharisees' response in verses 35-41.

12. What qualities do you think we need to have spiritual eyes that see?

13. How do you see "the works of God" displayed (v. 3) in this man's life in this passage?

14. When might have others seen God's work displayed in your life or the corporate life of your Christian community?

Pray: "Lord, give us spiritual eyes to see you and your work in the world. Help us believe. Where we experience spiritual visual impairment, help us to see and share you and your truth boldly."

NOW OR LATER

We know the man in this passage struggled due to his lack of vision, and Michael (described in the introduction) experienced suffering as well. God is working for the good of those who love him, even if sometimes it seems he isn't. Meditate on Romans 8, especially verses 18 and 28-39.

NINE

WE ALL HAVE GOD-GIVEN GIFTS

1 Corinthians 12:4-27

Two students at the University of Illinois at Urbana-Champaign, Barrett and Liam, met through an on-campus aquatic therapy program. They were paired together at random and soon grew to be close friends. Barrett, a wheelchair user, joined Liam at church and in InterVarsity Christian Fellowship.

A false and dangerous assumption often made, whether or not we are self-aware enough to realize it, is that those without a disability help and serve those with disabilities, and it is a one-way street. Untrue. We serve *alongside* each other as God gives spiritual gifts and talents to all his children.

God has given both Barrett and Liam spiritual gifts of leadership and leading musical worship, among other things. They have a mutual desire to reach out with Jesus' love to others in their area, including a God-given idea to host an adaptive boccia ball club called BocciABILITY. How fun is that?

Group Discussion. What type of talents and gifts get more attention in the church today, and why do you think this happens?

Personal Reflection. Ask the Lord to help you see the spiritual gifts he has given you *and* others in your community.

Many in the secular society in Corinth found significance in their abilities and talents by putting them on display. This continues within the church today; Paul addresses it here. *Read 1 Corinthians 12:4-27.*

1. What varies among different believers, and what stays the same?

2. Who gives spiritual gifts and why?

3. What are some of the gifts mentioned in this passage?

4. How does verse 11 pull them all together?

5. In verses 12-13, Paul mentions kinds of division prevalent in the early church (ethnicity and social status). What kinds of divisions or categories might affect the church today?

6. How does Paul get his point across about the church having many different parts?

7. What do you think happens if some of the parts are missing or trying to be something they're not?

8. As is often the case, God's Word tips things on their head: weaker parts are indispensable, and parts we give less honor actually have special honor. Why do you think God does this?

9. How might you see this reversal played out in your church or group?

10. How do you feel about your part in the body of Christ?

11. Does your perspective line up with how God wants you to think and feel about your place in his church?

12. What are some practical ways we can live out verses 24-27, especially as we consider accessibility or lack thereof in our fellowships?

Pray for yourself and others to be using your gifts and giving special honor to those with seemingly less honorable gifts. Ask the Lord to show you ways to advocate for yourself and others, especially those with disabilities, so their gifts can be seen, used, and valued within the body of Christ.

NOW OR LATER

To learn more about spiritual gifts read 1 Corinthians 12–14, Romans 12, Ephesians 4, or 1 Peter 4. Ask God to help you see more of his gifts in yourself and others, especially the gifts that are less acknowledged and honored.

LEADER'S NOTES

My grace is sufficient for you.

2 CORINTHIANS 12:9

Leading a Bible discussion can be an enjoyable and rewarding experience. But it can also be *scary*—especially if you've never done it before. If this is your feeling, you're in good company. When God asked Moses to lead the Israelites out of Egypt, he replied, "O Lord, please send someone else to do it" (Exodus 4:13). It was the same with Solomon, Jeremiah, and Timothy, but God helped these people in spite of their weaknesses, and he will help you as well.

You don't need to be an expert on the Bible or a trained teacher to lead a Bible discussion. The idea behind these inductive studies is that the leader guides group members to discover for themselves what the Bible has to say. This method of learning will allow group members to remember much more of what is said than a lecture would.

These studies are designed to be led easily. As a matter of fact, the flow of questions through the passage from observation to interpretation to application is so natural that you may feel that the studies lead themselves. This study guide is also flexible. You can use it with a variety of groups—student, professional, neighborhood, or church groups. Each study takes forty-five to sixty minutes in a group setting.

There are some important facts to know about group dynamics and encouraging discussion. The suggestions listed below should enable you to effectively and enjoyably fulfill your role as leader.

PREPARING FOR THE STUDY

1. Ask God to help you understand and apply the passage in your own life. Unless this happens, you will not be prepared to lead others. Pray too for the various members of the group. Ask God to open your hearts to the message of his Word and motivate you to action.

2. Read the introduction to the entire guide to get an overview of the entire book and the issues which will be explored.

3. As you begin each study, read and reread the assigned Bible passage to familiarize yourself with it.

4. This study guide is based on the New International Version of the Bible. It will help you and the group if you use this translation as the basis for your study and discussion.

5. Carefully work through each question in the study. Spend time in meditation and reflection as you consider how to respond.

6. Write your thoughts and responses in the space provided in the study guide. This will help you to express your understanding of the passage clearly.

7. It might help to have a Bible dictionary handy. Use it to look up any unfamiliar words, names, or places. (For additional help on how to study a passage, see chapter five of *How to Lead a LifeGuide Bible Study,* InterVarsity Press.)

8. Consider how you can apply the Scripture to your life. Remember that the group will follow your lead in responding to the studies. They will not go any deeper than you do.

9. Once you have finished your own study of the passage, familiarize yourself with the leader's notes for the study you are leading. These are designed to help you in several ways. First, they tell you the purpose the study guide author had in mind when writing the study. Take time to think through how the study questions work together to accomplish that purpose. Second, the notes provide you with additional background information or suggestions on group dynamics for various questions. This information can be useful when people have difficulty understanding or answering a question. Third, the leader's notes can alert you to potential problems you may encounter during the study.

10. If you wish to remind yourself of anything mentioned in the leader's notes, make a note to yourself below that question in the study.

LEADING THE STUDY

1. Begin the study on time. Open with prayer, asking God to help the group to understand and apply the passage.

2. Be sure that everyone in your group has a study guide. Encourage the group to prepare beforehand for each discussion by reading the introduction to the guide and by working through the questions in the study.

3. At the beginning of your first time together, explain that these studies are meant to be discussions, not lectures. Encourage the members of the group to participate. However, do not put pressure on those who may be hesitant to speak during the first few sessions. You may want to suggest the following guidelines to your group.

- Stick to the topic being discussed.
- Your responses should be based on the verses which are the focus of the discussion and not on outside authorities such as commentaries or speakers.
- These studies focus on a particular passage of Scripture. Only rarely should you refer to other portions of the Bible. This allows for everyone to participate in in-depth study on equal ground.
- Anything said in the group is considered confidential and will not be discussed outside the group unless specific permission is given to do so.
- We will listen attentively to each other and provide time for each person present to talk.
- We will pray for each other.

4. Have a group member read the introduction at the beginning of the discussion.

5. Every session begins with a group discussion question. The question or activity is meant to be used before the passage is read. The question introduces the theme of the study and encourages group members to begin to open up. Encourage as many members as possible to participate, and be ready to get the discussion going with your own response.

This section is designed to reveal where our thoughts or feelings need to be transformed by Scripture. That is why it is especially important not to read the passage before the discussion question is asked. The passage will tend to color the honest reactions people would otherwise give because they are, of course, supposed to think the way the Bible does.

You may want to supplement the group discussion question with an icebreaker to help people to get comfortable. See the community section of InterVarsity Press's *Small Group Idea Book* for more ideas.

You also might want to use the personal reflection question with your group. Either allow a time of silence for people to respond individually or discuss it together.

6. Have a group member (or members if the passage is long) read aloud the passage to be studied. Then give people several minutes to read the passage again silently so that they can take it all in.

7. Question 1 will generally be an overview question designed to briefly survey the passage. Encourage the group to look at the whole passage, but try to avoid getting sidetracked by questions or issues that will be addressed later in the study.

8. As you ask the questions, keep in mind that they are designed to be used just as they are written. You may simply read them aloud. Or you may prefer to express them in your own words.

There may be times when it is appropriate to deviate from the study guide. For example, a question may have already been answered. If so, move on to the next question. Or someone may raise an important question not covered in the guide. Take time to discuss it, but try to keep the group from going off on tangents.

9. Avoid answering your own questions. If necessary, repeat or rephrase them until they are clearly understood. Or point out something you read in the leader's notes to clarify the context or meaning. An eager group quickly becomes passive and silent if they think the leader will do most of the talking.

10. Don't be afraid of silence. People may need time to think about the question before formulating their answers.

11. Don't be content with just one answer. Ask, "What do the rest of you think?" or "Anything else?" until several people have given answers to the question.

12. Acknowledge all contributions. Try to be affirming whenever possible. Never reject an answer. If it is clearly off-base, ask, "Which verse led you to that conclusion?" or again, "What do the rest of you think?"

13. Don't expect every answer to be addressed to you, even though this will probably happen at first. As group members become more at ease, they will begin to truly interact with each other. This is one sign of healthy discussion.

14. Don't be afraid of controversy. It can be very stimulating. If you don't resolve an issue completely, don't be frustrated. Move on and keep it in mind for later. A subsequent study may solve the problem.

15. Periodically summarize what the group has said about the passage. This helps to draw together the various ideas mentioned and gives continuity to the study. But don't preach.

16. At the end of the Bible discussion you may want to allow group members a time of quiet to work on an idea under "Now or Later." Then discuss what you experienced. Or you may want to encourage group members to work on these ideas between meetings. Give an opportunity during the session for people to talk about what they are learning.

17. Conclude your time together with conversational prayer, adapting the prayer suggestion at the end of the study to your group. Ask for God's help in following through on the commitments you've made.

18. End on time.

Many more suggestions and helps are found in *How to Lead a LifeGuide Bible Study,* which is part of the LifeGuide Bible Study series.

COMPONENTS OF SMALL GROUPS

A healthy small group should do more than study the Bible. There are four components to consider as you structure your time together.

Nurture. Small groups help us to grow in our knowledge and love of God. Bible study is the key to making this happen and is the foundation of your small group.

Community. Small groups are a great place to develop deep friendships with other Christians. Allow time for informal interaction before and after each study. Plan activities and games that will help you get to know each other. Spend time having fun together—going on a picnic or cooking dinner together.

Worship and prayer. Your study will be enhanced by spending time praising God together in prayer or song. Pray for each other's needs—and keep track of how God is answering prayer in your group. Ask God to help you to apply what you are learning in your study.

Outreach. Reaching out to others can be a practical way of applying what you are learning, and it will keep your group from becoming self-focused. Host a series of evangelistic discussions for your friends or neighbors. Clean up the yard of an elderly friend. Serve at a soup kitchen together, or spend a day working on a Habitat house.

Many more suggestions and helps in each of these areas are found in *Small Group Idea Book.* Information on building a small group can be found in *Small Group Leaders' Handbook* and *The Big Book on Small Groups* (both from InterVarsity Press). Reading through one of these books would be worth your time.

STUDY 1. A TRUE PLACE OF BELONGING AND INCLUSION, LUKE 7:36-50

PURPOSE: To understand that Jesus cares about hearts, not appearances, and see how he forgives and includes us all.

Group Discussion. The Five Thresholds may be a great tool to use if your group includes those that are not yet Christians or new Christians. See Don Everts and Doug Schaupp, *I Once Was Lost* (Downers Grove, IL: InterVarsity Press, 2008), or "The Five Thresholds" on the InterVarsity website, https://evangelism.intervarsity.org/five-thresholds.

Question 1. Pharisees like Simon were members of a Jewish sect who interpreted the law of Moses so strictly that they often missed the heart and meaning behind the law and felt self-righteous or religiously superior to others. The woman was known as sinful—she may have been the town's prostitute—and therefore had a much lower station in life than Simon.

Question 2. It seems the woman understood her sin and was humble and even desperate. This posture and realization helped her come to Jesus even though it was a big risk and she was not invited to this meal. She lavished Jesus with love by extravagantly meeting his tangible needs. Alabaster jars were beautiful and expensive, as was the perfume.

Question 4. Simon judged Jesus in his thoughts. He thought that if Jesus truly was a prophet, he would never let this sinful woman touch him.

Question 6. It's easy for some of us to judge Simon and not see any ways we may be similar. Help the group to consider what they may have in common with Simon as opposed to vilifying him.

Question 7. Jesus truly saw and knew both Simon and the woman. There is no hiding from him. Be sure to discuss Jesus' response of forgiving the woman's sins and telling her that her faith has saved her.

Question 9. Simon made several errors by not washing Jesus' feet, not anointing his head with oil, and not greeting him with a kiss. The sinful woman did all this and more. Love is the response to forgiveness. Only as we realize the hugeness of our own sin will we truly appreciate God's forgiveness.

Question 10. The guests knew that only God could forgive sins, yet Jesus was forgiving her. Jesus was, rightfully, equating himself with God, and this surely astonished the Jewish guests.

STUDY 2. GOD CREATED US AND KNOWS US, PSALM 139

PURPOSE: To understand how big God is, that he knows us intimately, and that we are his wonderful creation. God loves us and accepts us completely, even as we are.

Question 1. The *NIV Bible Study Commentary* by John H. Sailhamer (Grand Rapids, MI: Zondervan, 2011) says, "David gives poetic 'theology' of God and his omniscience [all-knowing], omnipresence [present everywhere] and omnipotence [all powerful]" (221).

Question 3. It appears that David feels comforted and secure in realizing God is all-powerful, ever present, and all-knowing, as we see in his response in verses 6, 10, and 12. David's understanding of and close relationship with God is evident. For some group members this might not be the case. Provide space and understanding for different perspectives, yet feel free to share how these truths make you feel secure.

Question 4. I like how Dave Jenkins explains verse 14: "To be fearfully and wonderfully made includes every person from the womb to the tomb as human beings who bear the image of God. 'Fearfully and wonderfully made' means God intimately knows every person and all humanity belongs to Him" ("What Does Psalm 139 Mean by 'Fearfully and Wonderfully Made'?," August 13, 2019, Christianity.com).

Question 5. This could be an emotional question for some to answer; being looked down on, misunderstood, or treated as second best hurts deeply. Be prepared by listening well and empathizing. Also, the book *Changing Attitudes About Disability* by Dan Vander Plaats is a fantastic resource to help individuals and organizations talk through and change perspectives on disability (Sioux Center, IA: Dordt Press, 2020).

Question 6. Some ideas include meditating on and memorizing these verses, praying for and with one another to see ourselves as God sees us, and creating accessible spaces where friends come together to do this study and neither architecture nor attitude causes barriers.

Question 9. This is a hard concept for many of us. The *NIV Life Application Study Bible* (Wheaton, IL: Tyndale, 1991) is helpful here when it says, "David's hatred for his enemies came from his zeal for God. David regarded his enemies as God's enemies, so his hatred was a desire for God's righteous justice and not for personal vengeance" (1058).

STUDY 3. EQUAL ACCESS TO THE FATHER, EPHESIANS 2:8-22

PURPOSE: To understand that because we are saved by God's grace through Jesus' blood, we are all now brought near to God and should be one reconciled family without barriers between any people groups.

Group Discussion. Dr. Erik Carter's "Ten Dimensions of Belonging" wheel is a fantastic resource you may want to show your group as you talk through this question. See Elizabeth Turner, "Carter Explores What It Means to Be a Community of Belonging for People with Disabilities," *Notables*, May 24, 2019, https://notables.vkcsites.org/2019/05/carter

-explores-facets-of-true-belonging-inclusion-of-people-with-disabilities -in-our-communities.

Question 1. Prior to where we pick up in verse 8, Paul explains that all of us were "dead in your transgressions" (Ephesians 2:1). Verses 4-5 explain how Christ made us alive and say, "by grace you have been saved," just as in verse 8. We are saved by grace through faith, which is all a gift from God. Our response to God's grace is to do the good works he prepared for us to do.

Question 2. While the NIV describes us as "God's handiwork," the NLT says we are "God's masterpiece." We are each his work of art created to do the good works he has planned ahead of time.

Question 3. The former (pre-Jesus) status for the Gentiles was being outside of God's people. "They (the Gentiles) were then what many Jews would call 'the uncircumcision.' Circumcision was the seal of the covenant with Israel, and so what distinguished Jews from the rest of the world. . . . The Gentiles' exclusion from the community of God's people meant they had no part in the covenants which promised the Messianic salvation" (Max Turner, "Ephesians," in *New Bible Commentary* [Downers Grove, IL: InterVarsity Press, 1994], 1230-31). In dramatic contrast, now through Jesus' blood the Gentiles—and all of us—are brought near to God! For those who have ever felt excluded or separate, the truth in verse 13 is truly healing.

Question 4. Jesus destroyed the barrier and made the two groups one. Prior to Jesus, Jews and Gentiles kept away from one another. "Jews considered Gentiles beyond God's saving power and therefore without hope. Gentiles resented Jewish claims. Christ revealed the total sinfulness of both the Jews and Gentiles, and then he offered his salvation to both. Only Christ breaks down the walls of prejudice, reconciles all believers to God, and unifies us in one body" (*NIV Life Application Study Bible* [Wheaton, IL: Tyndale, 1991], 2133).

Question 6. As you lead by example, share honestly how you are doing personally with the Lord. This creates space for group members to do the same. For any in the group who have not yet started a friendship with Jesus, you could suggest they try something new like praying and asking God to show them he is real.

Question 9. Now (because of Jesus' death) we are all fellow citizens with equal status in God's kingdom! More personally, the Gentiles and all who believe in Jesus are part of God's household. This implies a special closeness to God as part of his family. Also implied in both these phrases is that no group of people is superior as members of God's kingdom or family.

Question 11. Reading Ephesians 1:22-23 might help put this passage about the temple and Jesus as the chief cornerstone into perspective. Isaiah 28:16 also refers to a "precious cornerstone." The temple is made up of many believers (past and present) joined together in one building, with Jesus being "the one from which the rest of the foundation is built outwards along the line of the proposed walls. The point would then seem to be that the temple is built out and up from the revelation given in Christ" (Turner, "Ephesians," 1232). This isn't about many individual temples but instead one temple made up of many individuals.

STUDY 4. WE ALL HAVE A PLACE AT THE TABLE, 2 SAMUEL 9:1-13

PURPOSE: To see how we can all be shown kindness and invited to sit at King Jesus' table as well as inviting others to do the same.

General Note: Disability language has, thankfully, improved over time. Some older translations of the Bible may use terms such as *crippled* in this passage. Today we might say Mephibosheth is a wheelchair user. Another example is with my son Luke, who doesn't speak but communicates with his iPad and in other ways. Today we wouldn't say Luke is mute but that he is nonverbal or low-verbal. The basic point is that language matters, and we need to avoid being derogatory. A great rule of thumb is to ask your friend with a disability what language they prefer and why. We all need to keep learning and growing, myself included.

Question 1. King David wanted to show kindness to Saul's family for the sake of his friend Jonathan. Read 1 Samuel 20:12-17, 23, 41-42 to see their deep friendship and the covenant David and Jonathan made to one another. In our passage David is fulfilling what Jonathan asked of him in 1 Samuel 20:14-15—to show kindness to him and his family.

Question 2. In 2 Samuel 4:4 we learn that Mephibosheth fell when he was five years old, and that caused his disability. Other folks in our passage include Ziba and his sons and Mephibosheth's son, Mika.

Question 4. As king of Israel, David held all the power. Saul's grandson Mephibosheth may have thought that David wanted to harm him, since when Saul was king he had repeatedly tried to kill David. Plus, "most kings in David's day tried to wipe out the families of their rivals in order to prevent any descendants from seeking the throne" (*Life Application Study Bible* [Wheaton, IL: Tyndale, 1991], 507).

Question 5. In biblical times (both the Old and New Testament) those with disabilities were often viewed as lowly, unclean, and even sinful. An example of this erroneous theology is shown in John 9:2, when Jesus' disciples say, "Rabbi, who sinned, this man or his parents, that he was born blind?" Jesus answers that neither sinned. We will explore John 9 in study eight.

Question 7. Eating at King David's table made Mephibosheth like one of David's sons. This gave him high status, power, provision, and protection.

Question 8. I like what Pauline A. Otieno writes: "David did three things to restore Mephibosheth and show the world his rightful place." Mephibosheth's self-esteem was restored when David showed him kindness, his identity was restored when his status and inheritance were returned, and he was restored to society by being among King David's family ("Biblical and Theological Perspectives on Disability: Implications on the Rights of Persons with Disability in Kenya," *Disabilities Studies Quarterly* 29, no. 4 [2009], https://dsq-sds.org/article/view/988/1164).

STUDY 5. A NEW PURPOSE FOR US ALL, LUKE 5:1-11

PURPOSE: To see how Jesus calls Simon, James, and John by meeting them right where they were and then giving them a new mission in life, and to apply this to ourselves individually and corporately.

Question 1. The Lake of Gennesaret is better known as the Sea of Galilee. It was known also as the Sea of Tiberias.

Question 4. Luke's Gospel suggests that Jesus became friends with Simon before this interaction: he previously had stayed at Simon's house (Luke 4:38). Simon Peter and the other fishermen knew the best chance of catching fish was at night in deep water, and here it was daytime in shallow water. Simon called Jesus "master" (teacher) when he agreed to do what Jesus asked, but after the miraculously huge catch of fish showing Jesus' power, "he was overcome by a deep sense of fear and unworthiness in the presence of someone who demonstrated heavenly power and was thus shown to be a holy person" (I. Howard Marshall, "Luke," in *New Bible Commentary* [Downers Grove, IL: InterVarsity Press, 1994], 989).

Question 8. Jesus gave them a new vocation—from fishermen to fishing for people. But they were just getting to know Jesus and starting on their journey with him, and we see them repeatedly confused by things Jesus does and says throughout the Gospels. So it seems they couldn't yet understand all that Jesus meant.

Question 9. As an aside, it's worth noting here that the unemployment rate for those with disabilities is much higher: 7.3 percent compared to the general population at 3.5. These stats from the Bureau of Labor Statistics are for 2019, prior to the Covid-19 pandemic, but a new analysis hasn't been done at the time of this writing. As a church body let's advocate for each other to find the work and purpose God has for each of us and level the playing field.

Question 11. Jesus asked Simon, James, and John to leave behind their family and their livelihood to begin their new adventure with Jesus. Sometimes he asks us to forgive those who have overlooked us or put us down. Or we may need to leave behind a sin or habit that is hindering our relationship with him. But encourage the group and yourself that he never asks us to do this on our own strength or go it alone. In the booklet *My Heart—Christ's Home* by Robert Boyd Munger (Downers Grove, IL: InterVarsity Press, 1986), the narrator shows the Lord around his heart so Jesus can settle down there, comparing it to coming into his home. He doesn't have the strength to clean out a closet but says he will give Jesus the key. Jesus opens the closet and cleans it out, bringing fresh air to the whole house.

Question 12. Notice how Jesus calls a group of fishermen and friends to follow him together. Especially in the United States we often miss the corporate call for a response since much of our culture is individualistic. One of many Old Testament prophets who asked for a corporate response from those in power and warned against God's judgment was Micah. The rulers, prophets, and priests in the capital cities of Jerusalem and Samaria were oppressing the poor. Today as we see ableism, racism, sexism, and other forms of oppression, how might we respond as a group to these issues? Micah 6:8 is a good verse to guide us: "O people, the LORD has told you what is good, and this is what he requires of you: to do what is right, to love mercy, and to walk humbly with your God" (NLT). It's also interesting that Micah promised restoration and a kingdom of peace for those who trusted God. And he prophesied about a ruler being born in Bethlehem (Jesus!) who would someday bring a kingdom that would last forever.

Question 13. Dan Vander Plaats explains in *Changing Attitudes About Disability*, "When we are approached by people with disabilities, we tend not to first imagine what they can do, but what they cannot do. We immediately absolve people with disabilities (and many other people who are different from us) from the work God called each of us to. We unconsciously refuse to co-labor with people who have disabilities, all because of unfair assumptions that actually *block people with disabilities from participating in God's kingdom work*" (Sioux Center, IA: Dordt Press, 2020), 59.

STUDY 6. A DIFFERENT KIND OF HEALING, MARK 2:1-12

PURPOSE: To see that Jesus' purposes in interacting with people go beyond physical healing.

Question 1. It may help to read Luke 5:12-15, which comes right before Luke's parallel account of the paralyzed man. This should help group members understand that the large crowd was present as news about Jesus' miracles spread.

Question 2. The paralyzed man had some great friends, but it's hard and humbling to ask for and accept help—especially in Jesus' day, when a common misconception was that those with disabilities or illnesses or their parents had sinned to cause it!

Question 5. Allow adequate time for group members to share and process past experiences here that might be painful. Good reminders include God created each of us in his image, as Genesis 1:27 tells us. His plans are far above our own.

Question 7. "The Pharisees were a religious party who placed great stress on strict observance of the law and the minute detailed regulations which had subsequently been added to it." The teachers of the law "were a professional class of lawyers and teachers who generally belonged to the Pharisaic party" (I. Howard Marshall, "Luke," in *New Bible Commentary* [Downers Grove, IL: InterVarsity Press, 1994], 989).

Question 9. In 2 Corinthians 12 Paul writes that he asked God to take away a thorn in his flesh. Instead the Lord said, "My grace is sufficient for you, for my power is made perfect in weakness" (2 Corinthians 12:9). Thus Paul decides to boast only in his weakness. God's power shining through our weaknesses is one answer to this question.

STUDY 7. FOLLOWING JESUS' EXAMPLE OF FORGIVENESS, LUKE 23:32-49

PURPOSE: To appreciate how Jesus continued to offer forgiveness during his crucifixion, see how others responded to him, and learn how we might follow his example of forgiving others.

Question 1. The Skull mentioned in verse 33 was probably a hill alongside the main road to Jerusalem.

Question 2. Our passage doesn't include all the abuse Jesus suffered; however, we read in verse 35 that the rulers sneered at him and insulted him. So did the soldiers in verse 36-37. Even one of the criminals being executed with him was hurling insults. Bystanders would also see soldiers dividing up Jesus' clothes and casting lots for them (a common practice among Roman soldiers, fulfilling a prophecy in Psalm 22:18; see John 19:24). This mocking and abuse is on top of the excruciating pain of being crucified on a cross.

Question 5. Jesus' welcoming response to the faith of one of the dying criminals is amazing. Help those in your group to see and understand that Jesus responds to each of us as sinners the same way. When we ask, he forgives us and gives us new life in his kingdom.

Question 9. Darkness covered the area for about three hours in the middle of the day. "All nature seemed to mourn over the stark tragedy of the death of God's Son." The tearing of the temple curtain in verse 45 symbolized what Christ accomplished on the cross. "The temple had three parts: the courts for all the people; the Holy Place, where only priests could enter; and the Most Holy Place, where the high priest alone could enter once a year to atone for the sins of all the people. It was in the Most Holy Place that the Ark of the Covenant, and God's presence with it, rested. The curtain that was torn was the one that closed off the Most Holy Place from view. At Christ's death, the barrier between God and man was split in two. Now all people can approach God directly through Christ" (*Life Application Study Bible* [Wheaton, IL: Tyndale, 1991], 1860-61).

STUDY 8. GOD'S POWER DISPLAYED IN A MAN BORN BLIND, JOHN 9:1-41

PURPOSE: To see Jesus display his glory through healing the man's eyesight and how the man comes to believe in Jesus, advocates for himself, and speaks the truth.

Question 1. Jewish culture at the time largely assumed the person or someone in their family had sinned to cause disability or illness. I think we often have this broader untrue theology today as well: *If I'm a good Christian, I will avoid hardship and suffering.* But how can this be true in light of all the suffering Jesus endured? In Eugene Peterson's *The Message* Jesus' response to the disciples reads, "You're asking the wrong question. You're looking for someone to blame. There is no such cause-effect here. Look instead for what God can do." I love that!

Question 3. Jesus asked the man to go wash in the pool of Siloam, which was fed by an underground tunnel from a spring outside the city walls. Jesus could have just healed his sight by commanding it to happen, so it seems significant that he spit on the ground, created mud from his saliva, and touched the man when he put the mixture on him. And might Jesus have given the man an action to take to show his faith?

Question 4. Belief versus unbelief is a big theme in this passage as people try to figure out Jesus' identity. "In chapter 9, we see four different reactions to Jesus. The neighbors revealed surprise and skepticism; the Pharisees showed disbelief and prejudice; the parents believed but kept quiet for fear of excommunication; and the healed man showed consistent, growing faith" (*Life Application Study Bible* [Wheaton, IL: Tyndale, 1991], 1895).

Question 6. The man had faith and shared what he knew! At first he didn't know who Jesus was, but he knew Jesus made him see. The parents let fear stop them from speaking the truth and advocating for their son. It seems growing faith in Jesus caused the difference.

Question 8. As the group thinks about this question it may help them to remember the Holy Spirit is the advocate of God's heavenly reality who advances God's cause. See John 16:5-15. As the Holy Spirit comes alongside us and reminds us of the truth and that we are not left alone, so we can do the same for others. What a big help and comfort that is.

Question 10. When Jesus heard that the man had been thrown out, he went to find him and then shared who he is with the man. Jesus is such a wonderful advocate. It is an amazing thing to remember that God is our advocate and wants us all to see who he is.

Question 13. God's work is displayed through Jesus healing the man's vision, but even more so in helping the man to have spiritual sight and faith in Jesus. Other important ways the group might discuss are how the man stands up for Jesus and for himself.

STUDY 9. WE ALL HAVE GOD-GIVEN GIFTS, 1 CORINTHIANS 12:4-27

PURPOSE: To understand that the Lord through the Spirit gives each of his children spiritual gifts for the common good. We are the body of Christ, we all play a part, and the seemingly weaker parts are indispensable.

General Note: Some of the group members may know and be confident in their spiritual gifts, while others may not. Remind them that God gives every one of his children at least one spiritual gift that the Holy Spirit decides on. Also be aware that group members may hold different opinions on spiritual gifts. Continue to steer the group back to this passage if things get too off track, and don't feel like you need to have all the answers! Some background about Paul's letter: "Instead of building up and unifying the Corinthian church, the issue of spiritual gifts was splitting it. Spiritual gifts had become symbols of spiritual power, causing rivalries because some people thought they were more spiritual than others because of their gifts. This was a terrible misuse of spiritual gifts because their purpose is always to help the church function more effectively, not to divide it" (*Life Application Study Bible* [Wheaton, IL: Tyndale, 1991], 2081).

Question 1. Isn't it fantastic how verses 4-6 say three times that the same Spirit/God/Lord gives the gifts? So God stays the same, but there are different gifts, different kinds of service, and different kinds of working.

Question 2. The Holy Spirit gives spiritual gifts. In this passage the Spirit is mentioned nine times. Gifts are given for the common good of Christ's body. Western culture can be very individualistic, so it can be hard for us to think collectively like this, but we need to.

Question 3. The gifts listed in verses 8-10 are *not* an exhaustive list. Other passages mentioning other gifts are listed in the "Now or Later" section.

Question 5. I like how *The Message* puts verse 13: "Each of us is now a part of his resurrection body, refreshed and sustained at one fountain—his Spirit—where we all come to drink. The old labels we once used to identify ourselves—labels like Jew or Greek, slave or free—are no longer useful. We need something larger, more comprehensive." This is not to say, however, that our cultural identities, our abilities, or being part of the disability community (among many other ways we identify ourselves) don't matter. They just pale in comparison to our identity in Christ and being part of his body and kingdom.

Question 7. Help the group think about their church or campus group and what types of people and gifts may be missing. Without all the parts of the body and gifts present it can't function, or at the very least it isn't working as God intended.

Question 12. One idea is to pray and ask God to help you see if one part of the body doesn't have access or is missing. Listen to those in the marginalized group, become allies, and roll or walk alongside them.

Deborah Meyer Abbs has worked for InterVarsity Christian Fellowship/USA for over twenty-seven years and has focused on disability inclusion for the last several years. She is also a coauthor of Life on the Spectrum, *a faith-based book written by and for parents who have children with autism.*

Deborah wishes to thank many friends who were so helpful in giving feedback for this guide. Extra special thanks to Kat Roffina, John Anderson, Robert Burdett, and Joy Sherfey.

WHAT SHOULD WE STUDY NEXT?

LifeGuide® BIBLE STUDIES

Since 1985 LifeGuide® Bible Studies have provided solid inductive Bible study content with field-tested questions that get groups talking—making for a one-of-a-kind Bible study experience. This series has more than 120 titles on Old and New Testament books, character studies, and topical studies. IVP's LifeGuide Finder is a great tool for searching for your next study topic: https://ivpress.com/lifeguidefinder.

Here are some ideas to get you started.

BIBLE BOOKS

An in-depth study of a Bible book is one of the richest experiences you could have in opening up the riches of Scripture. Many groups begin with a Gospel such as Mark or John. These guides are divided into two parts so that if twenty or twenty-six weeks feels like too much to do at once, the group can feel free to do half of the studies and take a break with another topic.

A shorter letter such as Philippians or Ephesians is also a great way to start. Shorter Old Testament studies include Ruth, Esther, and Job.

TOPICAL SERIES

Here are a few ideas of short series you might put together to cover a year of curriculum on a theme.

Christian Formation: *Christian Beliefs* (12 studies by Stephen D. Eyre), *Christian Character* (12 studies by Andrea Sterk & Peter Scazzero), *Christian Disciplines* (12 studies by Andrea Sterk & Peter Scazzero), *Evangelism* (12 studies by Rebecca Pippert & Ruth Siemens).

Building Community: *Christian Community* (10 studies by Rob Suggs), *Friendship* (10 studies by Carolyn Nystrom), *Spiritual Gifts* (8 studies by R. Paul Stevens), *Loving Justice* (12 studies by Bob and Carol Hunter).

GUIDES FOR SPECIFIC TYPES OF GROUPS

If you have a group that is serving a particular demographic, here are some specific ideas. Also note the list of studies for seekers on the back cover.

Women's Groups: *Women of the New Testament, Women of the Old Testament, Woman of God, Women & Identity, Motherhood*

Marriage and Parenting: *Marriage, Parenting, Grandparenting*